AMAZING SEX AFTER 60

Maintaining An Active, Healthy, Exhilarating Sex Life Throughout Your Senior Years

Life begins at 60! For many people, life doesn't end when they retire. They find they can pursue new interests and pursuits, and this certainly includes carrying on, and maybe starting, an active sex life.

There is no reason not to continue exploring the pleasures of sex even through old age. Having an active sex life into your 60's can benefit overall health. There are plenty of statistics to show this can help encourage a person to live a very healthy lifestyle, they eat better , exercise more, have a more positive and upbeat outlook of life in general.

The aim of this book is to assist you in carrying on a healthy sex life throughout your old age.

Discover that people in their old age can and should continue to have active, healthy sex lives for overall physical, mental and emotional well-being.

Find out what common health issues can deter you from continuing an active sex life and how to overcome these health issues.

Learn some safe sex concerns that may affect you. Find out where to get help for common sex issues of your age group by talking to your doctor or in the internet. Plus a whole lot more!

Don't let your age, or anything else for that matter, hold you back from relishing the many pleasures of life!

CONTENTS

Introduction 8

Statistics On Sexual Activity For Those Over 60 10

Tips For Enjoying A Healthy And Happy Sex Life Into Your 60's 13

1. Misconceptions On The Sex Life Of Older People 16

Medical Problems 16

Social Setbacks 17

Media Bias 18

Self-Perception 19

Sex Is Better At 60 20

2. Modern Day Sex 26

Alternative Sexual Lifestyles 27

Awareness Of Women's Sexual Needs 28

Open Talk About Sex 28

3. The Benefits Of Sex In Your Old Age 31

Health Benefits 31

Advice For A Healthy Sex Life 34
   Tips On Boosting Sex Drive As You Get Older 36

Dealing With Changes In Sexual Relationships 38

4. Basic Sex Education For Women 41

Revitalizing Relationships 42

Woman On Top Positions 43

Fellatio 45

5. Basic Sex Education For Men 47

Man On Top Positions 49

Cunnilingus 51

6. Loving Yourself 53

7. Health & Other Issues 58

Erectile Dysfunction 60
   Common Causes Of Erectile Dysfunction For Males Older Than 60 60

Loss Of Bladder Control 63

Menopause And Andropause 63
   How Menopause Can Decrease Sexual Desire 64

Diabetes 66

Cancer 67

Heart Disease 68

Environmental Situations 71

Common Sexual Problems For Older Women 73

8. The Help Of Medication 77

Viagra... 77

Eating Well And Exercise 78

Common Sexual Hang-Ups 79
    Are Prescription Medications A Good Option For
    Enjoying Sex In Your 60's? 82

Revive Your Sex Life After 60 By Natural Means 85

9. Doctor-Patient Sex Talk 88

Loss Of Libido 90

Pain During Sex 91

Discussing Sex Through The Internet 92

10. Safe Sex In Your Sixties 96

A Rise In Std's Among The Age Groups 96

Condoms 98

Common Std's 98

Safe Sex Concerns For Those Over 60 101

Conclusion..105

INTRODUCTION

Having sex into your 60's and beyond can help you feel younger.

When we are young we often proudly tell people just how old we are. That all changes though when a person gets older. However, you are only truly as old as you feel. Skip the skin cream if you want to feel younger as one of the best ways to do so is to have a good sex life. Some will argue that this isn't always possible due to not having a partner, but even masturbating when you are 60 or older will help you to feel younger.

Sexual activity helps to relieve tension in both the mind and the body. It is agreed that all adults can certainly benefit from that. A healthy sex life also helps you to feel good about who you are. There are few things in life that are as intimate between two individuals as having sexual relations. If you are true to the meaning behind your feelings then sex can only get better for you as you get older.

It may be hard for younger generations to understand how sex can get better with age. It has to do with the emotional connection that is found in the older years. We often take our relationships for granted when we are younger even if we truly do love those we are with. The physical as well as the emotional connect that can be made is what makes it that much more special.

You can feel younger having sex when you are past your 60th birthday and have some additional perks. For example you often don't have to worry about work schedules, taking care of children, or many other types of interruptions that can get into your way. There is also no longer a risk of getting pregnant and that can allow many couples to feel very free.

When you are young, you often can't imagine being over 60 and still having sex. It may seem like you are going to be so old. It really depends on your age when you start having such thoughts though. Keep in mind that your physical condition is going to affect how old you feel. Some 40 year olds physically feel older than many 60 years old. Staying active is going to be key to being able to still enjoy sex at an older age.

You may not have experimented much with sex when you were younger but still have the desire to do so. You are never too old to have fun with sex so let your partner know what your desires are. Chances are they will be very willing to comply with what you want to be fulfilled. Make sure you find out what they need as well so both of you can enjoy the activities and feel younger in the process.

Sex is an activity that people can really enjoy for their entire adult life. It doesn't have to stop just because of the number of candles on your birthday cake. While it is true that you won't hear as many 60 something people talking about sex, they are still enjoying it. There are plenty of statistics out there that reflect this. You can feel good about yourself as well as feel years younger if you are actively enjoying sex at this age and beyond.

Statistics On Sexual Activity For Those Over 60

You may be surprised by the statistics for those over 60 enjoying sex. Women aren't just sitting at home knitting while their men are out on the golf course. Instead they are enjoying each other physically and that is good news. More than half of all individuals who are at least 60 years of age are engaging in sexual intercourse.

You may be curious about how often this is taking place. 22% say that they engage in sexual activity at least one a week. 28% of them say that they engage in sexual activity at least one a month. When you consider how many people in our society fall into that age group then we have something great to look forward to.

Even with more than half of all people over 60 engaging in sexual activity, approximately 39% will tell you they want more. It could be that they aren't involved in a relationship right now that is going anywhere. Others may be looking for the right person to be intimate with but it just hasn't happened yet. You will find casual sexual encounters among those over 60 don't often happen as they do for those in their 20's and 30's.

Almost 95% of adults over 60 will admit in surveys to participating in the act of masturbating. Many believe this is something that older people don't do. Yet that isn't the truth of the matter at all. More males engage in masturbating over the age of 60 than women though. Many men say it helps them to be able to stay healthy and to get an erection when they do want to have sex with their partner.

However, approximately 75% of those that fit into this category will tell you that they are enjoying the sex they are having. They feel aroused, they feel desired, and they definitely are benefiting from the activity. Both men and women continue to be able to achieve an orgasm at this age. It may take longer to become aroused but the end result doesn't seem to have changed.

Almost all women who are over 60 will tell you that sex today is better than it was for them twenty years ago. Many of them are still with the same partner. They just find that they have more freedom in their life now when it comes to sex. They also have learned to better communicate to their partner what it takes to arouse and satisfy them.

Men are five times more likely than women to not be able to perform sexually due to medical problems. Heart disease is a problem that can affect both men and women in this age group. Yet men can also suffer from erectile dysfunction due to their various medical problems.

Both men and women in this age group may find that they don't seem to feel as attractive as they once did. 16% of them will tell you they don't have sex as often as they would like to because of it. They may wait until the conditions are right such as it being completely dark.

The statistics regarding sexual activity for those over 60 can be viewed as quite accurate. These days more people that fall into that age group are proud of their sexual activities. They are very willing to share that information with others who ask. They also take parent in online surveys where they can share opinions but still maintain their anonymity.

Based on this information, those getting older shouldn't be too worried about their sexual lifestyle. In fact, many people over 60 will tell you that they have a better sex life now than they did just 10 years ago. It may be due to how they now feel about their body or just a change in their routine. Regardless, sex over 60 is definitely something you can look forward to.

Tips For Enjoying A Healthy And Happy Sex Life Into Your 60's

The issue of older individuals having sex is becoming more common. Many believe this has to do with baby boomers out there that are more open to the topic. They don't find it to be as taboo as it once was. Also, women feel there is more equality in today's society than in the past. They are more open to talk about their sexual relationships instead of hiding them as they once did.

There is no reason to think you won't be able to enjoy a very healthy and happy sex life into your 60's as well. Keeping yourself feeling good now is very important regardless of what age you currently are at. If you aren't enjoying sex now in your 30's or 40's you need to be asking yourself why not. You need to be facing those issues so you can get better results from the activity.

It is important to have a commitment to your partner too. Both of you want to be able to continue enjoying sex into your 60's and beyond. It can be difficult when one of the people in the relationship isn't able to enjoy it or to perform. By looking out for the health of each other it is going to make it possible though.

You need to feel your very best if you want to enjoy sex at that age though. Getting enough rest and enough exercise is very important. Walking as a couple can allow you to have to time to visit and communicate. At the same time you will be promoting your health and a better sex life into the future.

Don't underestimate the value of eating right either. It can be great to try out new recipes that are good for you. Cooking as a couple can be fun and make it less of a chore. You will also find this keeps both of you healthy enough to continue enjoying sex as you are getting older.

If you don't have a partner when you enter your 60's you should be more receptive to the idea. Some individuals of that age group continue to be old fashioned. They aren't willing to have sex with someone until they are married. That is a different look than what today's society promotes. There is also the issue of protecting yourself against sexually transmitted diseases too when you are with a new partner.

Everyone should be seeing a doctor annually for a full check up. These appointments are essential as early intervention can help to prevent problems that lead to not enjoying sex. If you have any problems enjoying it before that annual exam is due then schedule another appointment. Your doctor can assist you with getting your sex life back to a place where you are happy with it once again.

It can take some patience in order to deal with problems along the way. There are many that affect both men and women. Being aware of the changes in your sexual behaviors is important. Be willing to talk about them with your partner so they know what you need. During the times when you can't enjoy sex, you can still enjoy other levels of intimacy with each other. This will help keep the passion alive and encourage the partner to seek the assistance they need.

Do your part to ensure you are able to enjoy a healthy and happy sex life into your 60's. There is no reason why that part of your life should stop because of your age. Staying active physically, staying connected emotionally, and even being social will all help you to really get the most out of it. Sex is a great way to share yourself with another person and you will likely want to continue doing so as you get older. Make sure you take measures now to ensure it is going to be a possibility for you.

1
MISCONCEPTIONS ON THE SEX LIFE OF OLDER PEOPLE

Well, the secret is out. The New England Journal of Medicine recently published a report breaking the news: A healthy sex life is not only possible, but quite commonplace, well into the golden years. Retiring from your job doesn't necessarily mean retiring from an active love life. The survey, performed in 2007, revealed that, of those ages fifty seven to seventy five, well over half had had sex at least once within the previous year. Older people tend to enjoy and desire sex just as much as younger people, and it's time to put the zany old preconceptions claiming otherwise to rest.

Medical Problems

The hindrances towards maintaining a rewarding sex life past a certain age are generally social and medical ones, though even these statistics defy the age old myths and misconceptions about impotence and dysfunction in the elderly. The New England Journal of Medicine's report showed that only one in two people over the age of fifty seven admit to suffering from a sex related health problem. The most common of these are erectile dysfunction, dryness and an inability to achieve an orgasm. Recent developments in medicine and therapy have more than made up for these problems, for the most part, so there's no reason that they should be a stumbling block.

Social Setbacks

The social setbacks to people over sixty having a rewarding sex life generally come, regrettably, from such trusted sources as family, doctors and caretakers, who can often buy into the myth of the asexual old geezer and be unsupportive of the social and personal needs of people past a certain age who have found themselves in the unfortunate condition of having to grow dependent on those around them perhaps more than they'd like to. Many doctors tend to jump to the conclusion that their older patients are electively sexually inactive.

Sometimes these professionals are just misinformed, other times, they might be trying to save themselves from a potentially embarrassing conversation. Either way, this tends to put it into the hands of the patient to bring the subject up at the next check up. Talking with those that help you in your daily life is also imperative, and you shouldn't be shy to ask family members to introduce you into their own social circles or help you get around to social gatherings.

Sadly, a major setback in maintaining a healthy sex life is the lack of a partner. Many people over sixty find themselves widowed with, personal health allowing, half a century of healthy, active life ahead of them. In this day and age, very few widows and widowers are willingly abstaining from sex to preserve the memory of their wife or husband. That practice probably stopped being commonplace sometime in the old west. However, to the one or two readers out there who are just that old fashioned; The last thing someone wants is for their untimely passing to leave their loved one forever unhappy and unfulfilled, and the only way to truly honor the memory of our dearly departed is to make the most out of the years we have left in our own lifetimes.

Media Bias

Perhaps to blame for the misconception that senior citizens aren't interested in sex is simply the unfair portrayal of what is attractive and what isn't attractive in the media. In general, the celebrities wearing skimpy bathing suits on the cover of popular magazines are thin, white and in their twenties, and those over sixty are just one of the many groups of people completely ignored by this kind of attitude in the media. However, there are still a number of older sex symbols who counter this, including Clint Eastwood, who manages to fit a love scene in most of his movies even into his early eighties, and Jamie Lee Curtis, who recently went topless for an issue of AARP magazine. Still, the deck is heavily stacked in favor of making older people, racial minorities, women and men of various shapes and sizes, and basically everyone but the pampered members of a very small minority feel as if they can never be as attractive as the ridiculous young bulimia victims gracing the covers of popular magazines.

Most people over the age of sixty don't need to be told that it's still possible to be attractive, to feel sexy and to desire a healthy and active sex life, but the association nonetheless perpetuates the stereotypes in the minds of an overwhelming majority of uninformed people. The important thing is to not let it get to you. Many seniors report that the tendency for society to remain ignorant and inattentive to the sexual needs of those over sixty rubs off on them, and some, in response to the endless discouragement provided by popular culture and those who don't have the facts, simply give up on maintaining a healthy sex life.

Self-Perception

The first step to a rewarding sex life is to acknowledge yourself as an attractive, desirable individual, and an important part of that is disregarding any discouragement that comes your way. If those gossip rags and celebrity magazines make you feel uncomfortable with your own image, just stop reading them. If the people around you find it ridiculous that you would still consider looking for a sex partner at your age, just tell them, quite frankly, that it doesn't matter what they think.

A healthy sex life is an important part of just about any rewarding lifestyle. Maintaining a healthy sex life past the age of sixty may seem like an uphill battle, and certainly, society unfairly places some stumbling blocks in the way, but to give up on such an important part of what it means to be human is, to be quite frank, just plain silly. If nothing else, a healthy sex life is a declaration that you're not nearly finished yet, that some of your best years are still ahead of you, and that you won't be content to simply sit around for the rest of your life waiting to kick the bucket.

Sex Is Better At 60

Sex has a way of making relationships difficult when we are younger. Many young people struggle with the issue of when it is the right time for them to start having sex. They may feel they have found the right person and then down the road wish they had waited for someone else to share that experience with.

Many people will tell you that having sex at a young age can certainly lead to some difficulties with relationships. One party may want it to be very casual while the other has fallen in love. There are hurt feelings and even unwanted pregnancies that have to be dealt with. Some may say that they don't want to think about sex and being older, but those over 60 will tell you it is different – and the love it.

They don't have to deal with all the same struggles as they once did. Most women over 60 will tell you that they don't have to worry about looks. They know that the partner they are with wants to be with them for more than just the hot body they have. They have accepted that their body has changed with time and they still enjoy having sex.

Men over the age of 60 will also tell you that the burden is off them to have the big muscles. They also don't have to try to perform all night long like they did in their younger years. With all of the stress off the issue of having sex, the couple can focus on making each other feel good. It is a completely different feeling than what they experienced before.

Both sexes will agree that sex at this age is about much more than just the physical side of things. It is a way to connect with someone they love, respect, and desire on a deeper level. Sex doesn't have to be the central theme of the relationship so there isn't any pressure for it to start taking place. They can take their time to get to know each other before they move on to that level.

For couples who have been together for a very long time, they often find as they move into their 60's that they have more time to spend with each other. This allows them to rekindle their love for each other that may have been pushed aside for many of the past years in their relationship.

You will definitely find these types of relationships to be built on great communication. They two people will really enjoy being around each other. They love to talk and to spend time together. Having sex is just an added benefit of them spending that time with each other. They can bring that level of communication that they value into the sexual relationship as well.

For those over 60, still having sex means that someone finds you to be desirable. This is very important to both men and women. It allows them to feel loved and cared for. It also allows them to have a level of intimacy that goes beyond just sitting close or holding hands with someone. That can help them to feel young and revitalized.

You will also find that as people get older they value their relationships more. Even though young couples may be in love, they may not fully realize the importance of their choices. Older individuals are able to see the connection of a good relationship both outside of the bedroom and inside of it. That is what keeps their passion for each other alive.

If you fit into the category of individuals who think it isn't going to be much fun having sex one you are 60, think again. Re-evaluate your attitude about it once you have read the material online for those who are in that age group and loving their sex life. Things are going to change but having sex in your 60's and beyond can be a completely new experience. It can be more rewarding in many ways then what you experienced at earlier times in your life.

So many women enjoy sex more when they are over 60.

There is often a belief in society that men enjoy sex much more than women. For many years overall this is true. Women often worry about issues such as pregnancy, they have their hands full with too many things, or they aren't happy with their body. Yet they continue to engage in sexual activities as a way to keep their partner happy. Women are very good at doing what is going to keep others happy. It is often a part of their very giving nature.

Some women continue to engage in sex during their life as they want to be able to enjoy it more. They may experiment with new methods as well as new partners. All the while though it may just be something they go through the motions of. Women often associate the act of sex with intimacy afterwards so they do it in order to get to that part of it.

It is often said that many women enjoy sex more as they get older. There are many researchers who will tell you it has to do with changes in the body. A woman may find it easier to have an orgasm when she is in her 30's. She may have come to terms with how her body looks or be with the same partner long enough to be very comfortable communicating what it is that she wants.

This results in sex becoming something that a woman can enjoy and look forward to when she is older. It has more to do with intimacy than with just being sexy for someone. Since sex isn't the core of the relationship when you are older than 60, the pressure is off a woman to look perfect and to perform perfectly. This can help it to be something enjoyable instead of another time when she continues to critic herself.

There is said to be a great deal of passion in the sexual aspect of things for older couples. This is because it focuses more on the feelings involved than just the act itself. The woman finds her partner is taking more time for touching and caressing which is exactly what women crave when it comes to sex.

All of this pampering and personal attention for women past 60 years of age may be something new. They may not have had such experiences with sex when they were younger. While most men won't admit it, they often focused on their own sexual needs when they were younger as well. Older men are known to be able to please a woman better.

More women are opening up to tell others how much they enjoy sex into their 60's and older. This used to be a taboo subject so it was just assumed that they didn't really participate in it or enjoy it. Yet that seems to be very far from the truth. Researchers have found that women will open up about their sexual activities when they are older if someone is directly asking the questions.

There are many reasons why women find sex after 60 to be extremely gratifying. They are able to continue to enjoy this part of their life regardless of their age. It is exciting to have the freedom to explore their sexuality. They also love the fact that their partner finds them interesting and wants to have sex with them. This can really help a person who is getting older to feel very good about themselves.

2
MODERN DAY SEX

It's hard to make all-encompassing statements as to how society views this or that at any given point in history, as different sub-cultures, regions and demographics may have held views that were in contrast to what the majority of a population felt at the time, and there are a lot of misconceptions the young people of today still believe about what life was like fifty or so years ago. In particular, the idea that, before Elvis Presley was on television, nobody ever, ever, ever talked about sex with anyone at all is a myth.

Certainly a lot of people in the western world were reluctant or even adverse to the idea of openly discussing sex with just about anyone, but all these age old dirty jokes and black and white pornography had to come from somewhere. Of course, even if the alleged prudishness of the first half of the twentieth century is largely exaggerated and embellished, it's hard to argue that the cultural changes that took place in the United States and throughout Europe in the fifties, sixties and seventies didn't make sex easier to talk about in mixed company.

Alternative Sexual Lifestyles

Most recently, a whole range of alternative sexual lifestyles have seen wider acceptance in western society, for better or for worse, and only the most prudish minority still cast judgment on consenting adults doing whatever they please in the privacy of their own homes and the only sexual behavior really frowned upon is that which is inarguably unhealthy, unsafe or irresponsible. In the past, for example, most homosexuals, practicing or otherwise, were wise to keep their true nature a secret.

More recently, there are only a few places left in the United States or Europe where a gay man or a lesbian woman can expect to be treated with unwarranted hostility, and there are even entire neighborhoods in most large cities where homosexuality is not only accepted by celebrated. The late 20th Century sexual revolution has created a cultural atmosphere where just about anyone, within reason, can find a community where their personal choices are accepted and they are allowed to be exactly who they feel the need to be in life. The long term effects of these developments can only be guessed at, but the idea of self-repression for the sake of social acceptance may eventually be a thing of the past.

Awareness Of Women's Sexual Needs

Perhaps one of the most important developments in this maelstrom of change has been wider acceptance of the sexual needs of women. Where in the past, in many western sub-cultures, women have been expected to be coy, to be indirect and play hard to get, and to tip toe around the subject of sex, women can now safely talk about sex in a direct manner with just about any trusted acquaintance without fear of being branded a tramp with loose morals. While some of the more puritan members of western society might find the practice of openly talking about sex to be offensive, the end result is that all this talk facilitates much, much healthier lifestyles and attitudes.

Open Talk About Sex

After all, how are you going to be aware of sexually transmitted diseases and other health risks if you can't talk about them with anyone? Open communication amongst a society is one of the easiest ways for that society to remain in good health, both physically and mentally. For women to be able to talk openly about sex, especially with their partners, allows for much healthier, more productive, and more efficient relationships to be maintained, with both partners being able to communicate with the utmost sincerely exactly what their needs are.

Whatever credit some of the more sexually evocative pop stars of the last twenty years may like to claim for themselves, one of the people who deserves a lot of thanks for the recent social acceptance of talk about sex is Dr. Ruth Westheimer. Author of such books as *Dr. Ruth's Encyclopedia of* Sex and *Sex for Dummies*, Doctor Ruth came to national prominence in the mid 1980's when she hosted a radio talk show and would regularly appear on late night television talk shows and discuss sex frankly with the hosts and other guests.

Westheimer, born in 1928, with her charming demeanor and frank humor, was a major component in bringing sex out of the bedroom (figuratively speaking) and encouraging people to talk openly about sex with their friends, with their doctors and with their partners. In particular, Westheimer focuses on the health aspects of sex, including measures of safe sex practice, and on the personal benefits of maintaining an active sex life.

All things considered, all this talk about sex in public is, in the end, for the better, and would seem like a necessary aspect of maintaining a productive society. Western society has definitely broken the ice at this point, and people are now free to talk about some very important issues that were previously considered taboo. People are able to come out of the closet and express themselves sexually without so much fear of being rejected by society or treated with outright hostility. In turn, the questions we have about sex and sex related problems can be answered, facilitating better health and a more rewarding life in general.

The main thing to keep in mind about sex in the early twenty first century is simply this: Don't be afraid to ask. To be perfectly frank, if your doctor or partner has a tendency to get sheepish at the idea of open, no holds barred discussions on sex, that's their problem, and they'll have to get over it.

3
THE BENEFITS OF SEX IN YOUR OLD AGE

The personal benefits of sex have been well documented. Besides the sensual and emotional pleasure and fulfillment derived from the act of sex, studies have shown that there are several health benefits to having sex on a regular basis, as well. In fact, a study published in the British Medical Journal in 1997 showed abstinent men to have twice the mortality rate of men who remained sexual active. It's hard to say exactly what benefits were so beneficial to the men who had sex regularly, because there are just too many benefits to having sex to keep track of.

Health Benefits

To list just a few of these benefits...

- **Reduced risk of heart disease**
  A study released in 2001 showed that men who had sex about three times a week cut

the subject's risk for stroke and heart attack by half.

- **Physical fitness**
  It was once said that the bed was the greatest exercise machine ever invented. Since sex is a rigorous and (usually) low impact exercise, sex is often recommended as a great way to stay in shape. A typical sexual encounter burns about two hundred calories, about the same amount of calories burned by running for fifteen minutes on a treadmill. Not to mention, the pulse rate more than doubles from an average of seventy beats per minute to an average of one hundred and fifty beats per minute when a person is aroused. The muscular contractions during sex work much of the body, including the pelvis, thighs, arms, thorax, neck and buttocks, toning and strengthening the muscles. Sex also increases a person's testosterone levels, in both men and women, which leads to a stronger musculoskeletal system, therefore, sex is an excellent preventative measure against osteoporosis.

- **Improved sense of smell**
  This one probably comes as a surprise to quite a lot of people. Production of the hormone prolactin surges right after intercourse. Prolactin causes stem cells in the brain to create new neurons in the

olfactory bulb, the part of the brain that focuses on smell.

- **Reduced depression**
  This one is generally regarding women, though the act definitely helps fight depression in men and women, there are more specific biological reasons for this in women. In a 2002 study following around three hundred women, it was shown that, amongst sexually active women, the ones whose partners did not wear condoms were in general less prone to depression than the others. The theory put forth is that this has to do with prostoglandin, a hormone which only exists in semen. When absorbed along the female genital tract, it is suspected to have a positive effect on the woman's hormones.

- **Better immune system**
  A study from the Wilkes University in Pennsylvania shows that having sex at least once or twice a week boosts your levels of immunoglobulin A, an antibody which supports the immune system. This results in getting colds or the flu far less often.

- **Better bladder control**
  Whenever you stem your flow of urine, the set of muscles at work are also put to work during sex, so regular intercourse can strengthen these muscles and improve

bladder control.

- These are just a few of the health benefits of sex, but studies have also shown subjects who have sex regularly to have better teeth, less physical aches and pains and to be less likely to suffer problems related to the urinary tract, the prostate, the kidneys and the bladder. Perhaps the best health advice a person can receive is simply to have sex regularly.

Advice For A Healthy Sex Life

Of course, the body must be kept healthy with regular exercise and proper nutrition in order for its owner to experience a fulfilling sex life. In fact, many of the most common sex problems have been found to be directly related to poor health and a lack of good nutrition. Lack of sex drive or lack of interest in sex, impotence, premature climax, sterility, fatigue and various other problems have been linked directly to poor diets and inactive lifestyles.

Sex is a big part of life, but it's only one part of life, and a person's whole lifestyle should be maintained properly in order for a sex life to be rewarding. In fact, even treating psychological sex problems relies heavily on proper diet and exercise. Even when the problem necessitates counseling, a healthy lifestyle is impossible to overemphasize.

The best health advice a person can receive is to eat as much fruit and vegetables, drink as much water, and get as much sunlight as you feel you can safely handle. In fact, while the daily recommended servings of vitamins may do for a minimalist lifestyle (or simply a lazy person), most nutritionists recommend as much as twice or three times what the government recommends. Sometimes a person will go into the fridge for a glass of orange juice and before they know it they've had half the carton in a single sitting. When your body needs more vitamins than its receiving, it's not uncommon for this need to become a craving, and for that craving to manifest itself subconsciously, like eating an entire bag of carrots without even realizing it or a ten minute walk in the sun turning into an hour long stroll.

That's not to say that sex is supplemental or superfluous to a healthy lifestyle. After a long relationship ends, a person may find themselves going through depression and gaining weight and getting sick more often, even if they're still providing themselves with plenty of nutrition and exercise. Nutrition, exercise and sex are three of the most incredibly useful tools to put towards maintaining a healthy, productive, active lifestyle, no matter what age you are.

Tips On Boosting Sex Drive As You Get Older

Maintaining your sex drive as you get older is very important to most people. Sex is a satisfying part of their lifestyle and not one they want to lose. It is normal for a person's sex drive to diminish some though as they get older. Specifically those over 60 may find it is harder to get into the mood or even to get your body to physically comply with what you want to do.

There are some things you can do though to help you maintain your sex drive as you get older. Living a healthy lifestyle is going to make a very significant impact for you so don't blow it off. What you choose to do today is going to affect your health and your level of sexual desire as you get older.

Eating a well balanced diet is something you should incorporate into your life. If you aren't doing it now, then start to make some small changes. As time goes on you will adjust to them and they will become a second nature to you. Consuming too much caffeine can be a problem. If you aren't getting all the vitamins and nutrients that you need from food, make sure you take a quality supplement.

Make sure you take the time to exercise at least 30 minutes each day as well. Walking is very common for older individuals as it is low impact but very good for the body. Get a companion such as a friend or even a dog that you can walk with each day. Some malls and other locations have indoor walking clubs too which are perfect when the weather turns cold.

Maintaining a healthy weight is very important to sex drive. A combination of a good diet with plenty of exercise will help you to be successful in this area. It will also help you to feel great about how you look. Too many people are inhibited about sex as their body has changed from what it once was. That is going to be a fact of life for all of us.

Being happy with your body is also important. Too many people start to notice all the small details as they get older. They will see every line and wrinkle on their body so they aren't comfortable during sex. They don't have much self confidence that they are desirable. They aren't able to let go and enjoy what is taking place because they are too focused on such details.

Reducing the amount of stress in your life is important as you get older too. The toll it can take on both your body and your mind is more than most of us imagine. Not everyone can be worry free when they are older though. If your finances or relationships aren't in the best format, it can be hard to get past it. Do your very best though to reduce as many stressful issues from your life as you can. It will certainly help with your sex drive because you won't be preoccupied with other things.

If you are healthy as you get older, you will be able to maintain your sex drive. Both men and women have the ability to be turned on sexually until a very late age in life. They also both have the ability to continue having orgasms into those later years as well. It all comes down to how fit a person is though both physically and mentally.

Age is merely a number though as anyone who is over 60 can tell you. Many of them continue to enjoy as wonderful of a sex life as others who are only in their 40's. It is something you can strive for in your own life as well. Make sure you are making healthy choices today though so you won't have too many issues that reduce your sex drive as you get older.

Dealing With Changes In Sexual Relationships

There are going to be some changes in a person's life as they get older, there is nothing that can be done about it. One of them is that your sexual relationship is going to change. For some people it is for the better and for others it leaves them wishing for their younger days. Those that seem to enjoy sex more as they get older often find that with the reduction of stress in their life they can get more out of it.

They may find they aren't exhausted anymore too because life has slowed down for them. They may be retired now so the daily grind of work isn't causing them to go to bed so tired they can't even think about sex. They have plenty of time to spend looking and feeling good. This means they can also spend more time with their partner.

As many individuals know, having a quality relationship on other levels with your partner leads to better sex. You may find that now that you have time to spend with each other on fun activities instead of just household chores you enjoy each other more. It can bring an entirely new level of intimacy to the bedroom for you as well.

Many people over 60 that are retired also travel. The excitement of seeing new places with someone you have a sexual relationship with can rejuvenate your sex drive as well. You may find new locations for the activity to take place is quite a turn on. Where you are and what activities you are enjoying can also play a role in that.

Not everyone will have such an increase in their sexual behavior though as they get older. Some people may really want to have sex more often but their body isn't cooperating. They may find it harder to get or maintain an erection for the act to take place. This can lead to a great deal of embarrassment as well as anxiety.

The body may just simply start to feel older and more worn down too. This can result in a person having less sexual activity than they did before. It can be frustrating when a person isn't ready for these issues to take place. Sometimes you can get results if you take to a doctor. Other times you will have to be able to come to terms with some changes in your sexual behavior that are the result of aging.

Talking to a counselor about it can be very helpful as well. Some older individuals become depressed when they find their sexual relationship isn't what it once was. They may blame themselves for it and need help to cope. Others may become angry at their spouse due to their changed feelings towards sexual activity. It is very important for the relationship to be open enough to discuss such matters.

Dealing with changes in your sexual relationship when you are 60 or older may not be your cup of tea, but you may find you have no choice. You may be pleasantly surprised to find that sex gets better for you as you get older. You may also find that the best is behind you. Yet you can still have a good time with it if you are willing to make some adjustments.

4
BASIC SEX EDUCATION FOR WOMEN

An important part of the sexual revolution of the 20th Century was allowing for women to be more sexually assertive than they traditionally have been in the past. Well with equal rights comes equal responsibility, and long gone are the days when a woman could rightly expect the man to always be the one who takes charge or initiates the encounter. These days, a woman has a right and a responsibility to be just as knowledgeable, just as giving, just as dedicated, and just as romantic as their partner.

Women no longer go into marriages expecting their husband to teach them everything they know, rather, both the husband and wife are expected to enter their marriage with some degree of knowledge already in their hands, and a willingness to learn and grow together as a couple. Obviously, it's hard to reach the age of sixty without having picked up more than a few tricks, but it's also not uncommon for a couple to be together for decades without ever learning more than a couple positions or thoroughly exploring each other's preferences and fantasies.

Revitalizing Relationships

Keep in mind that fancy tricks aren't really a solid means of reinvigorating a romantic relationship that's grown boring, but rather, a way of making the sex more fun than it's been in the past, making sex new again, giving yourself unexplored territory to traverse. Special positions and tricks are often recommended as a substitute for counseling or even divorce, in the more extreme cases, but a strong sexual relationship requires a strong personal relationship first and foremost.

Even those who regularly indulge in sex without romantic attachments will often report the sex as being significantly more rewarding when practiced with a partner whose company is enjoyable outside of bed, as well. No sexual technique is magical, and if your relationship has some serious problems, the only responsible thing to do is to try your best to work it out, perhaps with the aid of a counselor.

The author offers apologies for getting this chapter off on a downer, but it must be said that, as useful as these tricks are, one can't expect to instantaneously fix a troubled romance by moving efficiently and effectively from erogenous zone to erogenous zone like an emotionally unattached sex machine. That's not to say that great sex can't be an excellent incentive to work things out, of course, just that it takes much more than great love making skills to maintain a positive relationship.

There are plenty more things a person can try, do, or experiment with than can possibly be covered in this chapter, and readers should consult one of the many books that focus specifically on sexual techniques and positions in order to get a more thorough education on the art of sex. The following should, however, serve as a decent starter course at the very least, hopefully encouraging the reader to pursue their love-making education further.

Woman On Top Positions

Some men prefer to be on top all of the time. Sometimes this is thanks to valid (albeit selfish) reasons, as for many men, being on top is simply more physically fulfilling. There are some men, though, who simply aren't secure enough in their own self to allow their partner to take the dominant position. Many women actually don't mind, but women tend to report the sexual experience as being more rewarding when they're given some control over the proceedings. It's entirely up to personal choice, but the least a caring man can offer his partner is an opportunity to see how she likes being in charge.

- **Reverse Cowgirl**
  This is one of the basic woman on top positions. This position has the man lying

on his back with the woman facing away from him while mounting him. Women tend to enjoy this position, but some men may find it uncomfortable. In particular, men with smaller penises may find this position unfulfilling, awkward, or even impossible. However, if you find it to be feasible and satisfactory to both partners, it comes highly recommended. The woman can lean forward, back, or sit upright, depending on persona preference.

- **Chest to chest**
  As the name implies, this position simply involves the woman lying on her stomach atop the man. The legs are spread farther or held tight depending on personal preference. This is an excellent position if stamina is an issue, as it allows the woman to release pressure on the penis by spreading her legs, thus allowing for a longer encounter. Some men report this position as being ineffectual, though, as it sometimes doesn't provide nearly enough pressure. Like any position, the effectiveness of this one varies from person to person.

Fellatio

About ninety percent of the art of fellatio is all about the woman's attitude towards the practice. When a man finds a woman who honestly enjoys performing oral sex, all else he needs is food, water and shelter, and he's basically set for life. The power of good fellatio can't really be overestimated. Receiving enthusiastic oral sex is a validating experience that helps to build self esteem and eliminate personal insecurities.

Before you even begin, make sure your partner knows that you enjoy doing this. The act should generally be performed in a well lit room by an attentive 'performer'. Approaching the experience with any reservation or in a dark room where he can't see your approving looks is far less involving and far less validating for the man.

The majority of the attention should be focused around the head of the penis and the part connecting the head to the shaft, the corona, the most sensitive part of the penis. The shaft itself is far less sensitive, and yet, a misconception still persists that the shaft is the important part of the job. Never mind how the girls in X rated movies do it, a talented lover knows to focus her attention on the end of the penis. Many men enjoy stimulation of the testicles, as well.

The important thing to remember about fellatio is

really to just get intimately familiar with your partner's penis. Explore with your hands and mouth until you finally find his tender spots. It may take several nights before you become really good at it, but your partner will worship you when you get it right.

5
BASIC SEX EDUCATION FOR MEN

Thanks in part to the recent changes in western culture regarding sex and the relationship between men and women, there's no doubt that men can safely expect their current or potential female sex partners to be more assertive and vocal about their needs than they have at times in the past. The best advice a man can be given about providing his partner with a satisfying sexual experience is simply that he should listen as much as possible, pay very close attention to what the woman says and what she does, and ask questions if it seems necessary.

No matter how thorough, a book on sexual advice can never match the effectiveness of being a good listener and paying attention. Of course, if you're over sixty and have been married to the same woman for awhile, you probably don't need to be told about how important listening is to women, but that importance can't be overemphasized, so keep in mind that, while the following advice generally gets a positive response, results may vary, and a man should expect to have to talk to his partner about her own likes and dislikes before he can consider himself a master of the art of making love.

Chances are, if you're an attentive lover who's always been willing to try new things and you're looking for new tricks to surprise your wife of several years with, you'd be better off checking a larger volume dedicated entirely to sexual techniques and positions, as the one you're reading now only has the space to provide a sort of starter's kit to the uninitiated. Maybe some readers will find this preposterous, but plenty of couples go decades without ever putting more than a couple of basic moves in their repertoire. The following should serve as an introduction to the sexually under-experienced, but hopefully, might also provide a new idea or two for the seasoned expert.

Remember that there are really only so many different things a person can do in bed, and you could probably get through an inch thick sex manual in a few months to a year. Fancy sexual techniques alone can never be the backbone of a serious relationship, and while great sex can certainly strengthen a marriage, it can never really save one. Too often, sex tips are given as a sort of substitute for solid relationship advice, so the following tips should be taken knowing that, as important as sex is, serious problems should be worked through with the help of a counselor, not the help of a sex book.

Man On Top Positions

Chances are, you've already tried one or more of these, as the more traditional positions tend to have the man in the dominant position. While everyone may like to take to be on top so as to really take control of the situation, there are times when a man or a woman prefers to have pleasure given to them rather than having to earn it.

- **Rear entry, aka doggy style**
  This position has the woman on her hands and knees with the man mounting her from behind. Many couples enjoy this position for its directness and for how easy it makes it for the man to control the situation. Very few couples prefer it as a regular position, though, as there is a compromise of intimacy, given that the man and woman can't see one another face to face, and the position isn't always as pleasurable to the woman, since very little contact is made with the clitoris if the man's penis isn't very large. This position is advisable if you need to fit a quick encounter into a packed day, as a lot of pressure is put on both partner's genitals.

- **Scissors**
  This is a popular position for the fact that it grants both partners some control. The position has the woman lie on her back and raise one leg, with the man straddling her lower leg and entering beneath her upper thigh. The woman can use her leg to control the tempo. This position is considered very intimate, allowing the lovers to hold one another and kiss.

- **Spread eagle**
  The woman lies on her stomach and spreads her legs as the man lies atop her. This position is more intimate than rear entry, allowing the man to kiss the woman or nibble on her ears, but can be uncomfortable for the woman when the man is heavier or has an unusually large penis.

- **Armchair**
  This position has the man and woman holding one another as in missionary, with the exception that the woman is sitting on an armchair, sofa, or bed, with the man kneeling before her. This allows both the man and the woman to better control the thrust of the love making as either partner can grip the arms of the chair for better stability.

Cunnilingus

One of the most personally validating sexual experiences is receiving oral sex, but giving oral sex can be just as rewarding. To be perfectly frank, a lover is really only as good as their ability to deliver oral sex. The following should be taken as a suggestion of where to start if, for whatever reason, you've yet to really have any experience at the task of performing oral sex. Expertise at the art of oral sex can only really be achieved through hours and hours of practice, and the whole experience will be more rewarding when two partners have been together for awhile and really learned where one another's sensitive spots and preferences are.

A good idea is to start slow. Remember that you're making love, not fighting for your life, so there's no need to be in a hurry. In fact, you shouldn't even be working below the waist until you've spent a significant amount of time in foreplay. Over sixty doesn't necessarily mean the same thing as "days are numbered", so act as if you have all the time in the world for your lover. Even if you've spent an hour kissing her body everywhere but between the legs, don't just go right for the clitoris, focus on her labia and everything else that registers a vocal or physical response.

Gentleness is generally appreciated, so relax your tongue and employ a soft touch when using your hands, but make sure to listen to your partner. Every woman is built differently and thinks differently and changes her mind often, so treat each time like a new experience, never stop listening and asking questions and trying new things.

6
LOVING YOURSELF

In a recent interview, sixty four year old actor R. Lee Ermey openly discussed his own masturbation habits. Discussing the art of leaving something to the imagination, he said "If you have an imagination anywhere near what mine is like, I mean, I still masturbate for Christ's Sakes! I can still visualize Marilyn Monroe and the Playboy bunnies from the 1950s", so consider the secret as being completely out in the open, everybody knows that sixty year olds still masturbate!

Still, a recent survey asking people over the age of fifty about their sex lives resulted in a lot of open, honest answers on a wide variety of topics, but the one subject where most participants declined to answer was masturbation. It may be the self indulgent nature of the act that makes it such a taboo subject of conversation for so many people, and many people are reluctant to talk about it even with their doctors or partners. Whatever your feelings on masturbation, rest assured that everybody does it, with very, very few exceptions. In fact, the minority of the human population who don't indulge in masturbation tend to have suffered some sexual trauma in the past or to have been raised to harbor a negative opinion of sex in general.

Masturbation is not a sign of perversion as it was considered in the 19th Century when doctors would patent anti-masturbation chastity belts and the like, but rather, a sign of a healthy sexual appetite and an acceptance and appreciation of one's own body. Masturbation practiced by a person in a sexually active relationship is just as healthy and as common as masturbation practiced by single people, and the act should be seen not as a substitute for sex so much as sex with one's self. It may sound corny, but many people prefer to refer to masturbation as "making love to one's self" or "self love" rather than by more vulgar terms.

Masturbation has been proven to have plenty of benefits to a person's health. In men, ejaculation and heightened arousal help release epinephrine, which many professionals cite as a hormone which helps to relieve depression and stress. Ejaculation also helps to prevent prostate cancer. Masturbation is recommended as a way to ensure regular ejaculation, where sexual intercourse can be inconsistent thanks to times where the partners must be separated for some reason or during periods of living single.

Masturbation is also noted as a way to maintain the balance in a relationship wherein one partner has a higher interest in sex than the other.

It probably doesn't even need to be said, but the statements released by doctors and ill-informed hypothesists in the 1800's were largely unfounded and in the long run proved completely foolish. The only health risk involved with masturbation is soreness. In fact, it even helps with reproduction, as, in men, masturbation ensures that fresh, lively sperm reach the egg rather than sperm that have been laying around in the urethra for awhile.

In love making, masturbation can be very useful. A person who masturbates regularly can be expected to have a better knowledge of their own personal likes and dislikes, a more intimate knowledge of their own sexual identity, and as such, sex will be all the more rewarding. Mutual masturbation is also a common and intimate form of sexual intercourse. This simply involves a couple using their hands to stimulate one another rather than having traditional intercourse.

While it may seem to be somewhat impractical to make a habit of this, many experts recommend treating masturbation as a form of sex to the extent of including foreplay and ambience in the experience. Most people honestly just don't have the time for that, or may feel ridiculously self indulgent, but the sentiment is a valid one. A person should treat their body with respect in all regards and consider masturbation as a way to take care of one's self.

Unfortunately, a lot of people simply masturbate out of compulsion or boredom without really taking the time to enjoy the experience. You might not really want to bother lighting candles and putting on soft music every time you feel the urge to pleasure yourself, of course, but masturbation should certainly be regarded in a positive manner rather than the traditional view which has generally deemed the practice vulgar at best and punishable by death within certain puritan communities in the 18th century.

The most common reason for masturbation is, of course, to satisfy one's sexual cravings during times of single living. Many people over the age of sixty find themselves in the unfortunate position of being widowed or recently divorced or otherwise living on their own for the first time in years or perhaps ever. During such times, regular masturbation is an excellent solution, but it should be viewed as a temporary one. Being single and over sixty is no excuse to become a recluse or to give up on ever finding another lover.

Most experts recommend that women employ the use of sex toys. Even outside of masturbation, such items can be of assistance during sexual intercourse, though some men can grow insecure if the toys are larger than their own equipment. If you'd rather not venture a visit to an adult book store, these can be bought discreetly over the internet. It hardly needs to be said, but pornography can be viewed privately in your own home over the internet, as well. Some people may still prefer the local color provided by the area sex shops, but the privacy and selection provided by the internet has been liberating to the many people out there who are too shy to ever set foot into a store that specializes in porn movies and dildos.

7
HEALTH & OTHER ISSUES

It's a sad fact of life that no matter how well you take care of yourself, no matter how strict your diet and how regular and thorough your exercise routine and how frequent your doctor visits, a person's health starts to deteriorate past a certain age. Needless to say, this can result in some changes in one's lifestyle, sometimes requiring simple fixes like wearing a hearing aid or taking regular medication, but in extreme cases, a person can suffer major limitations in basic abilities. Luckily, it's pretty easy to stay out of a wheelchair and keep from becoming a crippled old fogey as long as you take good care of yourself (a note to women, drink plenty of milk to help prevent osteoporosis), but even so, disease and injury can come from plenty of other sources besides a poorly maintained lifestyle.

Sometimes disease is hereditary, or a person can suffer major injury just by being in the wrong place at the wrong time. Whatever the cause, it's not uncommon for people over sixty to have to make compromises in their lifestyle, compensating for personal health that's not what it used to be. As long as you're not comatose, though, there's never excuse for one of these compromises to be the elimination of your sex life. Even if you suffer from a condition that is sexual in nature or one that directly affects your sexual activity, as long as you're conscious and breathing and still experience the desire to live an active sex life, there's just plain no such thing as a good reason to give up on sex.

For singles, the main thing is simply to be up front and honest with a new partner about any health conditions you suffer from that might directly affect the experience. It's not an easy thing to make it into your sixties without developing a single recurring health problem, so it's nothing to be embarrassed about. Understandably, it can be difficult to convince yourself of that when it comes time to talk about it, but if you will yourself into a sincere discussion about the changes your body has gone through in recent years, you'll probably find it to be far less an embarrassing conversation than you'd expected.

The following is intended to provide some advice on how to deal with common health problems with relation to one's sex life. Any major conditions that have not yet been addressed should be discussed in depth with one's doctor and with one's sexual partner.

Erectile Dysfunction

Before you go running to the doctor to get a Viagra prescription, keep in mind that erectile dysfunction is not strictly a problem for men over sixty. Even men barely out of their teen years can experience regular erectile dysfunction. Oftentimes, erectile dysfunction is a result of a deficiency in vitamins and other vital nutrients. As stated earlier in this volume, before going for some medical aid, it might be wise to try a change in diet and exercise habits first. This is perhaps the most common problem for men, and one of the more potentially embarrassing should it occur at an inopportune moment, but luckily, it's also one of the most easily remedied.

Common Causes Of Erectile Dysfunction For Males Older Than 60

Erectile dysfunction can definitely hurt a man's physical and mental ability to enjoy sex. Even if he is turned on by a woman and wants to complete the act, the body simply isn't going to comply. This is an event that just about every single man out there will experience at least once in their life, especially as they get older. It isn't a big deal unless it is happening on a regular basis.

The key to getting past it though is to realize that you aren't alone. Too many men hide their issue with erectile dysfunction from everyone. They are too embarrassed to tell their partner so they may look for reasons to avoid sexual activity. They can pick fights, become distant, and even make the partner feel bad about their appearance to cast blame in another direction.

For those not in a serious relationship, erectile dysfunction can prevent it from occurring. They know that eventually a new relationship will get to the point where sex should be taking place They don't want any women to find out they can't perform so they withdraw from women in a social setting all together.

It is important for men to realize that there are many common causes for erectile dysfunction. Therefore there is no reason to feel inadequate about the process taking place. It is going to be a natural part of getting older for many men. A doctor can often help to identify what the cause of the problem is though and help a man get his sex life back.

Vascular disease accounts for more than half of all the erectile dysfunction cases in males over the age of 60. This has to do with the arteries to the penis getting blocked and so not enough blood can get to it for a full erection. This is a condition that can often be treated though.

Smoking is a common issue that can lead to it as well. Males who smoke more than a pack of cigarettes per day are at the highest risk. Stopping to smoke can make a huge difference for the individual in just a month or two.

There are a variety of medical problems that can lead to erectile dysfunction for men. The biggest one though is diabetes. The nerved and blood vessels to the penis may be damaged and so there isn't enough blood that is allowed to flow into it for an erection to take place.

When we hear about hormone problems and sexual behavior for those over 60, it is mostly associated with women. Yet approximately 5% of all males suffer from some type of hormone problem. That is what is responsible for their problems with getting an erection. They may have a problem with their kidneys or liver due to hereditary illnesses or excessive alcohol use.

Some men fail to product enough testosterone as they get older so they need a supplement to help with their sex drive. There are also times when traumatic experiences can affect the normal ability to get an erection. It could be due to an injury that harms the spine or even due to the onset of various diseases that affect the central nervous system.

Doctors have to be careful about prescribing medications for various ailments as well. All prescription drugs have side effects and hundreds of them have impotency as one of them. Since many of these drugs have to be taken on a daily basis it is a huge concern. These various medications may be to treat heart disease, diabetes, depression, or anxiety. It is important for a doctor to try to find a good medication that works but doesn't affect the ability to obtain and maintain a natural erection.

With all the technology available today, that is no reason for a man over 60 to suffer from no sex life. There are simply too many ways in which they can be helped. However, this help can't be offered unless they are open and willing to discuss their sexual problems with professionals.

Loss Of Bladder Control

Another problem that commonly causes embarrassment but is also easily remedied. Strengthening bladder control can be done with Kegel exercises which, as stated earlier, occur naturally during sex or when stemming off the stream of urine, or can be done by tensing the muscles while sitting or standing in one place for an extended period of time. Another obvious solution is simply to not load up on too many fluids before sex.

Menopause And Andropause

Menopause and andropause (when older men find their bodies producing less testosterone) can result in lowered sex drive. This is another problem that can sometimes be fixed with a change in diet, but more often than not, some medical attention will be required. Luckily, there are pills and shots readily available by prescription which can help to improve hormone levels.

How Menopause Can Decrease Sexual Desire

There are some significant changes that take place in a woman's life. One of them is menopause. This marks the end of her ability to conceive a child. There will be no more menstrual cycles once the woman is in complete menopause. Yet it can take years to go from the start of menopause to completely finishing it. Most women start the process around 45 and finish around 60. It can be sooner or later though as each woman is different.

There is a common misconception that women who have gone through menopause no longer have any sexual desire. They may continue to engage in the activity to keep their partner happy, but they don't get any pleasure out of it. This is certainly not the truth though.

Many women over the age of 60 are involved in very fulfilling sexual relationships. They love not having to worry about their period. They also don't have to worry about an unwanted pregnancy very late in life. This new found freedom for them means they are able to fully focus on the act of sexual activity and not the various repercussions of it.

Some women do experience a drop in their sexual desire though after menopause. Many women experience problems with the vagina being dry after menopause. This can make it hard for them to get pleasure out of sexual activity. There are some great products on the market though that will allow you to moisturize the vagina without any negative side effects.

It is a good idea for a woman with such issues to see a gynecologist for a complete evaluation though. They may be able to help come up with a natural remedy that can prevent ongoing issues having to be addressed with it. For many women, dealing with vaginal dryness can cause a mental block with sexual intercourse.

They may connect it with being undesirable now that they are in their 60's. This low self confidence can cause women to shy away from sexual intercourse as well. Being able to really enjoy your body and your sexual desires when you are over 60 is very important. It will encourage you to do what you can to be able to bring back a high level of sexual desire to your life.

Sometimes something over the counter though isn't enough for a woman to get back the sexual desire she once had. Your doctor may offer you supplements of hormones in the form of estrogen.

Since the level of it in the body drops dramatically due to menopause, replacing it definitely can be helpful.

Menopause doesn't have to hinder your sex life though for women over 60 years of age. If you enjoy sex and you want to continue doing so, there are remedies out there that can help. Don't be embarrassed to discuss the issue with your doctor either. They deal with such issues all the time. They will know how to help you get back to where you want to be sexually.

For many older couples, menopause can throw a wrench into what was once a very enjoyable part of their intimate relationship. It is important to discuss what has taken place. A woman doesn't want her partner to assume the lack of sexual responsiveness has anything to do with them not being attractive anymore. Find a good solution that works for you so that menopause won't stop you from engaging your sexual relationship.

Diabetes

One of the lesser known facts problems with diabetes is erectile dysfunction. High blood sugar can cause blood vessel and nerve damage which adversely affect sexual responsiveness. High cholesterol can slow blood flow thanks to fatty deposits. If there's an upside to this, it's that improving the quality of one's sex life can be an excellent incentive to watch one's blood sugar levels.

Cancer

Of particular interest is cancer. Testicular cancer, prostate cancer, cervical cancer and even breast cancer can all affect a person's sex life adversely. Even if a cancer survivor is lucky enough that the effects of the cancer aren't immediate in a physical sense to their sexual ability, the emotional trauma of losing a breast or a testicle can be devastating and damage one's self esteem, leading to loss of interest in sex and even complete inability to perform.

It goes without saying that the best way to fight cancer is by prevention and early detection. As mentioned earlier, an active sex life can help prevent testicular and prostate cancer, keeping those parts of the body active and discouraging tumors from forming. Women should check themselves regularly and consult their physician about any unusual abdominal cramps or aches. Intimate foreplay can also double as a form of checking one another for cancer. Any abnormalities in your partner's body should be brought to their immediate attention.

The loss of self esteem that might occur after invasive surgery or amputation is natural. It's difficult to look in the mirror and see a body that isn't the one you're used to and it's easy to think that this means you're less of a man or less of a woman than you were before. Prosthetics are often provided after amputation and every major city in the civilized world should have a support group that fits your needs or a therapist well equipped to help cancer survivors. An interesting trend for women who have lost a breast to cancer is to skip the breast implant and get a tattoo in its place. Given the health problems associated with breast implants and their appearance, which many women (and a surprisingly high number of men) find distasteful, the tattoo option has grown in popularity as a declaration of identity and as an empowering way to exert some control over the appearance of one's own body.

Cancer shouldn't ruin one's sex life, and getting back to business as usual is one of the most life-affirming ways to deal with the emotional trauma of undergoing invasive surgery (once the scars have healed and you've returned to your normal self, of course). Those that haven't suffered through cancer or helped a loved one through the treatment and recovery process can't pretend to know exactly how those directly affected by cancer will feel, but good advice for anyone who's suffered such intense emotional trauma is simply not to let it run your life.

Heart Disease

Heart disease is one of the biggest killers of both men and women in our society. It is very important to take care of it. One fear that many people over the age of 60 have is that their heart disease will put a damper on their sex life. There are ways to effectively control your heart disease though and still be able to enjoy a very active and fulfilling sex life.

Heart disease can result in a person having to take medications for the duration of their life. Many of these medications have proven to be successful but not without a cost. There can be various side effects with them such as erectile dysfunction. This means a male can't maintain an erection. Most doctors won't prescribe various types of medication to help with it such as Viagra or Cialis though if you don't have a healthy enough heart to be engaging in sex in the first place.

Of course there is the common fear in our society that anyone who has heart disease could die due to the excitement of sex. There have been reports of heart attacks and other issues occurring during sex for those with heart disease. While these instances do occur, they are often very few and far between. Still, if your doctor tells you to change your habits and that you can't engage in various types of sexual activities you need to listen.

In most instances though, your sex life doesn't have to come to a screeching halt. Instead you may find there are some modifications to be made. You need to be open to the suggestions and the changes though as they may prove to be more satisfying to you than you thought. Remember that your overall health is very crucial and so you need to be disciplined about sticking to the set boundaries by your health car professionals.

Make sure you are following all of the orders like you should. This means taking daily medications on time. Eat meals that are healthy for you so that you can keep up your energy. Pay attention to signs from your body that something just isn't right. If you get dizzy or short of breath during sexual activities then you may need to stop what you are doing.

Having a loving and caring partner through all of this is extremely important. That can help to reduce your level of stress and anxiety. They should be willing to forego various types of sexual activity in order to help you stay as healthy as possible. You may find that making various changes to your lifestyle though helps. You may be able to resume old forms of lovemaking in the future if you are willing to stick to such necessary changes.

Heart disease is a very serious issue and you should do all you can at a young age to prevent it from occurring. You want to be as healthy as you can when you get into your 60's and beyond. It will ensure you have a happier lifestyle that also includes being able to enjoy various types of sexual activities.

Should you end up with heart disease though due to poor lifestyle choices or due to heredity, you can still find ways to enjoy sex. It is important to discuss the issue with your doctor though. You certainly don't want to be engaging in any types of behavior that aren't in your best interest.

Environmental Situations

Some individuals really have a fear of getting older. They don't want to be viewed by society as a "has been". They aren't really sure what their future holds so they tend to dwell on it. They may have memories of their own parents or grandparents with difficulties as they got older. It is only natural not to want to follow along that same path.

If you want to have a great sex life after the age of 60 then you need to really think about it now. What is your current sex life like? Do you enjoy the activity or do you just go through the motions? Are you in a serious and committed relationship that you would definitely like to still be involved in when that time comes?

Some people in their 30's and even their 40's put sex on the back burner. That is understandable with all of the various commitments we often have in our lives. People are on the fast track and over committed. There are family issues, career, and trying to find some time for yourself. It can leave a person drained and with two people on different schedules it is even more difficult.

Many researchers will tell you that the type of sex life you have in your younger years will influence how it is for you after 60. So if you aren't happy with what you have now you need to make some changes. Finding ways to be very happy with your own sexuality is very important. The number of people who aren't sexually happy is very high, yet very few of them are willing to express what needs to change to their partners.

Part of the problem though is the attitude that earlier generations had about sex. Many women still feel that it is their duty to please their man. Therefore they don't talk openly about wanting more or less sex. They don't express their desires of what they want to see happen. Since no one is bringing it up, their partners just assume they are pleasing them.

If you find that your life is one I mentioned about being too full for sex, then you need to cut back. Make a commitment to make sex something that is important in your relationship. It shouldn't be the only thing you have going, but certainly a perk. If you and your partner are having to pencil each other in for sexual activities then changes need to be made sooner than later.

Some individuals over the age of 60 find that their living conditions can become an issue as well. You may be ready to go to some type of assisted living facility rather than to live on your own. Are they going to approve of sexual activities taking place there? It is important to know what those guidelines are. Some places such as nursing homes don't allow it and there certainly is very little privacy.

Even if you end up living with your adult children in your older years, are you going to be comfortable with sexual activities? Many adults don't want their children to know about it even though they aren't little kids any more. The issue is further compounded when the parent living with them is dating instead of actually married.

There are many common issues to consider if you want to have a great sex life after 60. The main focus needs to be on what is going to make you and your partner very happy. There is no reason though not to enjoy sex if it is something you find to be important. You may have some barriers to deal with along the way, but with some accurate information and openness you can find solutions to them that will work well for you.

Common Sexual Problems For Older Women

Sex can continue for women at any age, but there are some common problems that can affect those over 60 and make it uncomfortable. If you aren't feeling good during the activity of course it is going to be something you avoid being a part of. That can really make you feel less attractive and even older than you really are. Sex is a big part of who we are even though it isn't the most important attribute.

Too many women just sum up these common problems as the end of a very happy sex life. Others never really enjoyed it anyway so now it is just one more issue to prevent them from considering sex as something wonderful or rewarding. Yet you don't have to let problems prevent you from enjoying sex after age 60. There are many things you can do to make yourself feel better.

Stress can be a huge factor that affects enjoying sex. Some women that are older find that they have things taking place in their life that overwhelm them. Dealing with that stress is very important though to help move on from it. Talking to friends or a professional counselor can certainly be helpful.

A change of partners can be difficult for women as well. Most women are very loyal to their partner and so it can be hard to become intimate with someone else. They may have gotten divorced later in life and just now came back onto the dating scene. Some women have lost their spouse due to death. After being with the same person for decades it is certainly a new experience to have sex with someone different.

Many women will find that it does take longer to become sexually aroused when they are in their 60's. Instead of being frustrated by this a woman just needs to find ways to work with it. Having a relaxing bath with a partner, a nice romantic dinner, or just cuddling for a while can help. A woman needs to make sure her partner understands what will arouse her as well.

The ability to naturally lubricate the vagina can be an issue as well. This is important to address because it can result in sexual stimulation as well as intercourse being painful. There is no reason for a woman to have to deal with this but many suffer in silence. They try to avoid the atmosphere for sex to take place so they don't have to discuss this with their partner.

It is often the result of the vaginal walls becoming thinner as a person gets older. The younger a person is when they go through menopause the more common it is that will occur. Women need to discuss such issues with their gynecologist before they just reach for an over the counter product to assist them with lubrication issues.

Even though women over 60 can end up experiencing some problems, most of them can be overcome. There are very few women who can't end up with a very satisfying sex life as they get older. You may have to work in order to physically and mentally get to that point though. Let your doctor help you too by being willing to share such issues with them. They are professionals so you shouldn't be embarrassed turning to them for assistance.

8
THE HELP OF MEDICATION

After a certain age, and depending on the individual's lifestyle and personal history, it may eventually come to pass that a person is put in the unfortunate position of having to rely on medical supplements and the like in order to attain an active lifestyle, and that extends to the bedroom. Most obviously, just about everyone who hasn't been living under a rock for the last decade or two knows about the little blue pill; Viagra.

Viagra

For all the cheap jokes Viagra has elicited from stage comics, it has nonetheless been an invaluable help to thousands and thousands of men over the age of sixty. In fact, upon being approved by the FDA, Viagra sold more in its first two weeks than any other medicine ever has in just fourteen days.

Some men who suffer from erectile dysfunction opt to suffer in silence though. Perhaps too embarrassed by their condition to discuss the possibility of taking Viagra with their partner or doctor, or simply too prideful to admit to needing the help of medication.

Erectile dysfunction is maybe the most common of all of the treatable problems that can seriously afflict a person's sex life, but is far, far from being the only one. The most important advice a person can be given in regards to dealing with a sexual dysfunction is simply this: Don't be ashamed. As difficult as it can be to admit that your body isn't as capable as it was even ten years ago, the initial hurdle of opening the dialogue isn't nearly as trying as spending your next forty years wrestling with frustration and loneliness.

Eating Well And Exercise

The first step to treating something like erectile dysfunction or loss of interest is, as stated in earlier chapters, simply checking your dietary habits and lifestyle. This book may be beginning to sound like a broken record, but it can't be said enough times: Eat well and exercise. Poor diet and an inactive lifestyle are at the source of just about every common health problem. If simply eating a little more in the way of fruits, grains and vegetables, and cutting back on smoking, caffeine and alcohol can solve your problems, there's no need to seek medication.

Common Sexual Hang-Ups

Of course, there are plenty of exceptions to the rule of diet and exercise. It's hard to tell someone with serious injuries or who is suffering from cancer that they'll be all better if they walk a few laps around the block every morning. The most common sexual hang-ups related to lack of proper diet and activity are fatigue, or lack of energy, erectile dysfunction, lack of interest and depression, but even these are quite often caused by something else. In the event that the need for medical aid becomes imperative to the activity of your sex life, the following is intended as a brief list of what you can talk with your partner or doctor about as a potential means for treatment.

- **Erectile dysfunction**
  As mentioned before, Viagra is the most well known and one of the most efficient ways to deal with erectile dysfunction. In fact, it's become so popular that even those who don't suffer from erectile dysfunction have taken to using the pill to enhance the sexual experience (no responsible doctor would ever recommend this, though). While it's been a godsend to sufferers who had previously all but given up hope, it's far from being the first or only method of treating erectile dysfunction. Some of these are inconvenient and unpleasant, however, for example, Alprostadil, which is injected

directly into the penis, and BEFAR, which is only sold in parts of Asia. With the existence of Viagra, a lot of these have become outdated, and for obvious reasons. However, counseling can be of quite a bit of help, and is often recommended to be tried prior to looking into Viagra. Erectile dysfunction is often the result of some psychological cause, and discussing the problem with a therapist can accomplish a few things to aid in the process of dealing with erectile dysfunction. Most obviously, psychological causes can be worked out and medical measures won't even wind up being required. If the cause is not psychological, counseling can help to rule out any subconscious hang-up, or it can be used to deal with any distress that comes as a direct result of the dysfunction.

- **Decreased libido**
  Decreased interest in sex is probably the sexual dysfunction most commonly chalked up to "old age" and then just left untreated. Many people aren't even bothered by their own declining libido, but given that this text is, after all, dedicated entirely to the subject of sex after the age of sixty, it can probably be assumed that this does not describe the reader. A list of every last one of the various causes of decreased libido would fill a one thousand page encyclopedia all on its own, so this chapter, unfortunately cannot list

them all. However, just as with erectile dysfunction, lack of interest in sex often relates directly to psychological trauma suffered in life. Sometimes, the stress involved with the aging process is enough to do this to a person all on its own. This should probably be your first line of defense after examining your lifestyle.

- **Sleep apnea**
A surprising cause, but one to think about if you have already ruled out psychological hang-ups, is sleep apnea. This is a condition wherein a person will stop breathing for as much as ten to thirty seconds at a time while sleeping. Research is still pending on the issue, but it is suspected to be a cause of lack of interest in sex. Treatment is fortunately quite simple. Doctors who diagnose patients with sleep apnea will usually prescribe a mouthpiece to wear to bed which holds the lower jaw in such a position as to open the airway and allow for easier breathing. As awkward as it sounds, the result is increased energy and a sound night's sleep.

- **Arthritis**
Some people might not think of this one, but anyone who's suffered from serious arthritis knows just how bad the condition is in terms of limiting a person's lifestyle choices. Luckily, this is one of the most

easily treated, in many cases. For minor arthritis, pain relievers and physical therapy should allow for better mobility and comfort in bed. Unfortunately, those who suffer from more intense arthritis might have to look into measures as extreme as surgery to replace broken joints. Resting and staying fit with low impact exercise are pretty much required no matter how serious or minor your arthritis, though.

Whatever your situation, the most important thing is to confront whatever is standing between you and a healthy sex life, head on and to never give up on living your life exactly as you see fit.

Are Prescription Medications A Good Option For Enjoying Sex In Your 60's?

While a person's mind may still want to have a strong and active sex life the body may not always be able to comply. There are some prescription medications out there that have proven to offer those over 60 help with such issues. For example those with diabetes or arthritis may find that they are in too much pain or don't have enough energy for sex.

However, with medication to control their diabetes and a good diet their energy levels increase. There are medications for arthritis too that can prevent the joints from swelling up. This means a person can go about activities including sex and not be in constant pain. It may be something that younger generations take for granted, but when you are physically in pain it can be almost impossible to enjoy the pleasures of sex.

One of the most common types of prescription drugs that men use to help them enjoy sex is Viagra. This is a type of pill that a man takes when he is mentally excited to have sex but the penis isn't getting or maintaining an erection. Many men have found Viagra and similar products have allowed them to have a very enjoyable sex life once again. Their age hasn't been able to stop them from making this important element part of their normal lifestyle.

The pill known as Cialis has also become very popular. This is because a man can take it and then be able to maintain erections when he is ready over the course of the next 36 hours. This means you don't have to plan the act of lovemaking such as you do with Viagra and similar types of prescription medications. It allows the process to be more natural and many men really enjoy having that control over their sexual activities.

There are similar types of prescription medication for women as well. One huge problem for them after menopause is a decrease in the hormone estrogen. As a result they may find they have very little interest in sex. Even if they engage in the act, they just aren't getting the level of pleasure out of it as they once did. Estrogen pills can be prescribed to help a woman gain her libido back.

Prescription medications may be a good option for you if you are older and you really want to improve your sex life. You will need to talk to your doctor about it so a complete assessment can be performed. Identifying the true reasons why you struggle to get an erection or why you aren't enjoying sexual activity is important so be honest with your answers.

There are certainly plenty of prescription medications offered today to help those over 60 be able to continue with a healthy and satisfying sex life. Keep in mind that some of them are a quite expensive though. There are also some side effects associated with each of them to be ready for. You may have to experiment with a variety of different types of prescription medications before you find the one that helps you get to the level of sexual activity you want in your life.

Prescription medications aren't the answer for everyone though. There may be too many health issues for you to consider using them. You may also find that the various side effects also make it difficult for you to enjoy sex. Never use prescription medications for someone else because you are too embarrassed to talk to your doctor about it.

You do owe it to yourself though to see if there is medication that can significantly improve your sex life into your 60's and beyond. There are plenty of people out there in this age group and beyond that find sex more enjoyable now than any other time in their life. Being able to continue engaging in the activity helps to keep them both healthy and happy.

Revive Your Sex Life After 60 By Natural Means

If you want to have a better sex life later in life then you do now, you can work to rejuvenate it. When was the last time you really took some time to pamper yourself? If it has been a while then take some time to do so. Go get a new outfit and a hair cut or color. Buy some new make up and plan a romantic dinner for you and your partner.

Allow yourself some time to fantasize about sex during the day as well. Take a nice warm bath before bed. You can picture what you will do with your partner when you are done with the bath. Leave them a detailed note in the morning about plans for the evening. It can certainly make a huge difference in the way you see each other romantically. Keep it fresh and alive so that no one gets bored with the sexual activity that is taking place.

Take a look at your mental well being as well. If you aren't in the best of moods then do what you can to perk yourself up. Sometimes seeing a professional counselor can help you out as well. Sometimes there are issues not dealt with in the relationship that lead to tension and resentment. If you can get them on the table and out of the way your sex life will likely improve.

Taking care of yourself physically is important as well. Don't let yourself get lazy or overweight. Stay active and eat well so you can stay at a healthy weight. You may need to work with a dietician to plan healthier meals. It is never too late in life to make such lifestyle changes. It does take some planning and commitment but your will find there are many great benefits from it.

Get rid of those nasty habits such as excessively drinking alcohol. In the long run it will lower your sexual desire and performance, especially for men. Smoking is also a factor that will become more of an issue as you get older. Being comfortable in your own skin and with how you look is a great way to get you in the mood to initiate sexual activity with your partner as well. They will find it to be a tremendous turn on that you are attracted to them.

Sometimes just changing the location of where sex will take place can make it better. If you are always doing the act at home, take a weekend vacation to some place romantic. You can also use a different room in the house to spice it up a bit. There are books on new positions and even on romancing your partner to look at as well. You may find talking honestly with your partner about how to please them can really make a difference.

There are herbal pills for both men and women on the market as well. Since you can buy them over the counter at most health food stores people assume they are 100% safe to take. Still, you need to consult with your doctor first. You may not be healthy enough to engage in sexual activity. You certainly don't want to risk your health for sex so getting a full assessment from a professional is the best place to start.

9
DOCTOR-PATIENT SEX TALK

One could write a thousand page volume on all the problems that arise when unfair stereotypes are attached to a person. The unfortunate presumption that people over sixty still persists pretty strongly in the minds of the uninformed, and one of the biggest problems people past sixty might have to deal with is getting their doctor to talk with them, openly, about problems and concerns regarding sex. This is especially true with younger doctors who, for all their expertise, simply lack the life experience to know what questions need to be asked and what needs to be said.

These stereotypes mean that, unless you luck out and get a doctor who is either old enough to know that retiring doesn't mean eliminating your sex life, or simply smart enough not to fall for those dumb clichés, the responsibility to "break the ice" is going to rest squarely upon the patient's shoulders, and even then, you might find the doctor is reluctant to get too involved in the subject.

Even if you don't have any particular concerns or nothing seems immediately threatening, it's very important to talk to your doctor about sex now and then so as to discuss preventative measures and proper lifestyle habits regarding your sex life.

Even if you've already broken the ice or you know your doctor to be comfortable talking to you about sex, make sure to keep the dialogue open and uninhibited. There really aren't any taboo questions when it comes to your health, nor are there any dumb questions. In fact, any doctor in the world could tell you a dozen stories about symptoms that seemed minor but were in fact indicative of a much larger problem. Just as detectives can solve a crime with a single fingerprint, a good doctor can identify a serious problem from a single, seemingly minor symptom.

It should also be noted how important it is to get a second opinion any time the first opinion comes from a doctor who seems disinterested (it may also be time to get a new doctor if yours treats you with disinterest). Plenty of people have narrowly avoided serious debilitation and even death by acting on their concern when the initial diagnosis was carried out with what seemed to be indifference or boredom. Even if this sounds like it's encouraging a kind of paranoia and you don't want to be seen as some distrusting old geezer, this is your health we're talking about. As long as you're not a diagnosed hypochondriac, there's never a good reason to ignore the concerns you have about your own body.

Loss Of Libido

One of the most common problems confronted by people over sixty regarding sex is the loss of libido. If you find yourself losing interest in sex, here are some a couple simple questions to ask your doctor:

- **"Could it have something to do with the medication I've been taking?"**
  There are many, many medications on the market which inhibit the libido, and even in the event that you aren't taking any medications that affect the sex life on their own, sometimes, two or three can combine in the body to create such an effect.

- **"Is my lifestyle to blame?"**
  Outside of the obvious diet and exercise solution, loss in libido can also be caused by excessive stress in your daily life or even a generally disappointing day to day routine. Your hormone levels rely heavily on your emotional state and it's important to take care of yourself in every area of your life you want to have a healthy sexual appetite.

Asking more general questions can help, but communication with your doctor should be as direct as possible and you should give him or her as much information as you can in order to get the most precise answers.

Pain During Sex

Another common problem is experiencing some degree of pain during sex. This has a pretty wide range of causes, so make sure to be as specific as possible about where the pain is and how it feels, no matter how embarrassed you might feel when delving into such explicit detail. Again, when it comes to your health, there's never a good reason to be ashamed or embarrassed.

For women, vaginal pain is quite often caused by dryness, which can occur when there isn't enough time before penetration for the woman to become sufficiently aroused. This can generally be treated without the help of a doctor if the woman is simply willing to discuss the problem with her partner and request that they dedicate more time to foreplay during sex. Another problem can be lowered estrogen levels. If more foreplay doesn't solve the problem, your doctor may prescribe supplemental hormones.

When a man experiences pain in his genitals during sex, in can be indicative of any number of problems and should be dealt with immediately. Sometimes, soreness during or after sex is thanks to something relatively minor like eczema, fungal condition, or simply dryness (in which case, just drink more fluids or see the above paragraph), but at times, it can be thanks to much more serious problems. Even minor aches and pains in the penis and especially the testicles should be diagnosed as soon as possible.

Other examples of pain experienced during sex can be due to arthritis. Since sex exercises parts of the body in ways almost exclusive to the sex experience, it's not uncommon for a person to not even know they suffer from arthritis until having sex. Even if simple over the counter medication seems to eliminate the pain, this should nonetheless be discussed with your doctor, as minor aches and pains can be indicative of developing problems that may worsen over the years.

Discussing Sex Through The Internet

The generation gap is alive and well when it comes to many issues in our society. Sex is one of them and so the older generations are turning to the internet as the perfect place to feely talk about it. There younger co-workers, friends, and certainly their own children don't want to discuss it with them. It can be hard for younger generations to accept the fact the their own parents and even grandparents are still having sex.

Yet more and more people are living a healthier lifestyle to late in life. This means there is no reason why someone over the age of 60 can't be having the time of their life when it comes to their sexual relationships. It doesn't matter if they have been with the same person for years or if they are newly on the market and seeing what it has to offer them.

Not everyone from the older generations is comfortable talking openly about sex. They may feel guilty or embarrassed about doing so. Yet with the internet you can talk freely to others and hide behind the screen. No one ever has to find out your real name or what you look like. You may be talking online with people in another country or just across town from you. The anonymous nature of the internet though makes it safe and so people tend to open up more.

There is a great deal of information to be found online too about how sex is for those over 60. Individuals who are experiencing low libido or a variety of other problems that are sexual in nature can find out more about it. They can get support because they know that they aren't alone in what they are going though.

In many instances, reading such information can help them come to terms with where they are. They may be encouraged to go see a doctor or a counselor to help them get passed the issue. They may find that they are able to rid themselves of the guilt associated with having sex with a new partner after their previous one died. All of these issues and more are covered in great detail online for those that are 60 and older.

A person can simply choose to read articles that are posted online. Search engines are a great way to be able to narrow down the topics. As you read more articles you can jot down notes. This way you can come up with more keywords to enter and do other searches on. You can collect the information you want from the privacy of your home without feeling self conscious about it.

There are also plenty of forums where other people can read your posts and respond to them. This is a great way to get personalize information that is specific to the questions you have. You can also do your part by reading what others need and responding. This is a great way to give back the support that has been given to you along your road to sexual happiness at an older age.

It seems that there are more and more individuals older than 60 out there sharing their stories of having sex. Some of them are fun while others are full of questions. You do need to make sure that you get reliable information though. Just because there is something written on the internet doesn't make it true. Take the time to verify the resources. Keep in mind that a great deal of the information you do come across will be the personal opinions of other adults and not based on anything credible by and expert.

Still, what you do get from other people who have been through similar experiences can give you something to think about. It can help you to overcome personal fears as well as provide you with some comical relief from time to time.

10
SAFE SEX IN YOUR SIXTIES

Sexually transmitted diseases are spread through the exchange of bodily fluids. This can include vaginal fluids, semen, pre-ejaculate, and blood. Before having unprotected sex, it's a good idea to get blood tests for both yourself and your partner. Sexual contact should also be avoided if you or your new partner have any open wounds or are simply unsure of your own sexual health.

A Rise In STD's Among The Age Groups

A study released in the nineties estimates that at least one million people contract a sexually transmitted disease every day. These statistics are startling. Most recently, junior high and high school education as well as some specific college courses have begun making an effort to educate young people about the dangers of venereal disease. There have also been multi-million dollar ad campaigns to raise awareness, but all this education and information has been aimed squarely at people under the age of twenty five, who make up more than half of the people in the world who carry a sexually transmitted disease.

A group that is quickly catching up with people under twenty five with regards to catching these diseases may surprise you: People over sixty.

This is thanks to a number of things. For example, the fact that all this education tends not to be aimed at people past a certain age, so the only people who seem to get a free education about safe sex are those under the age of twenty five. Many older people see sexually transmitted disease as something that doesn't affect them and many of the old stereotypes about those in their sixties and older affect the way society treats the problem. The people making efforts to educate the world about AIDS, HIV, proper condom use and other concerns would seem to be falling for the classics, such as that anyone over thirty is only having sex with their wife or husband of several years, or is simply sexually inactive.

A more surprising source of this boom in STDs for older people is menopause. More specifically, the way certain women behave after going through menopause. Many women who have practiced safe sex all their lives to avoid pregnancy will opt to stop using condoms after menopause, assuming that since they can no longer have children, there's no need to use contraceptives.

Condoms

The widespread use of latex condoms was almost unheard of in some social circles until relatively recently. While the latex condom has existed since 1912, many people stuck with clunky, outdated methods until the last few decades. Some misconceptions still persist, however.

For the longest time, condoms were made from animal intestine. These were highly ineffectual. Today, lambskin condoms are still being produced. The makers usually claim that these aid in sensitivity, but to be frank, a lambskin condom is about as effectual as wet tissue paper.

The first rubber condom, invented in 1844, was pretty unappealing, as well. Having been two millimeters thick, with stitches going down the side like a football, and being very expensive (though fortunately, it was reusable!).

A couple of notes on correct condom use; never use oil based lubricants, as these can eat erode the latex, rendering the condom useless, and don't apply the condom too snugly. Stretching a condom tight over the penis may be an excellent way to show off, but a tightly applied condom is more likely to burst or tear during intercourse or ejaculation.

Common STD's

A brief list of some of the more common sexually transmitted diseases and how to avoid contracting them is as follows:

- **HIV (Human Immunodeficiency Virus)**
  Estimates as of the time of this writing have it that 0.6% of the entire world population is infected with HIV. HIV can nowadays be treated, to some extent, and likely won't kill you unless it mutates into AIDS.

- **AIDS (Acquired Immune Deficiency Syndrome)**
  In 2007 alone, AIDS claimed more than two million human lives, with an estimated 33.2 million people living with the disease worldwide. AIDS cripples the immune system to the extent that so much as a common cold can become a fatal disease. There is no way to tell if a person has HIV or AIDS just by looking at them or by asking them or even by looking at a list of their previous sexual partners. It's never, ever a good idea to have unprotected sex with a new partner without being tested. Condoms can protect both partners to an extent, but even condoms cannot guarantee that the disease will not be passed form partner to partner.

- **Herpes simplex**
  Herpes simplex makes itself known in the

form of painful and irritating sores on the genitals. Luckily, there are treatments on the market that help to limit outbreaks of these sores even once you've contracted the virus, but this shouldn't be seen as a license to act irresponsibly. A common misconception is that a carrier of this virus has to be suffering an outbreak during the time intercourse takes place for the disease to spread. Nothing could be further from the truth. It's possible to catch herpes at any time. Luckily, contracting herpes is easily preventable by proper condom use. Besides the physical ailments, herpes has actually been implicated in the development of Alzheimer's disease.

- **Gonorrhea**

    This can be a hard disease to diagnose as it might go without showing symptoms for as much as a year after contraction. In fact, it's estimated that around half of the women who carry gonorrhea are completely asymptomatic, or sub clinical, in which case, the infection will only show itself in minor ways, such as difficulty urinating on occasion or minor vaginal discharge. In men, gonorrhea can cause swelling and pain in the testicles and prostate.

Some years ago, penicillin was a sort of miracle drug and it would cure most cases of gonorrhea in short time. However, people in many parts of the world have built up an immunity to penicillin, and other antibiotics must be used. Exactly which antibiotic will have to be determined by a doctor, as exactly which antibiotic should be used depends on local information of resistance patterns.

Luckily, gonorrhea is also preventable by proper condom use, but in the event of contraction, some strains have proven strongly resistant to drugs.

Safe Sex Concerns For Those Over 60

Just because you get older, it doesn't mean you can be careless about your choice of sexual partners. For those over 60 years of age, you want to do your part to protect yourself. Both men and women need to take the responsibility for having condoms readily available. While they risk of pregnancy is likely in the past, the risk of sexually transmitted diseases is not.

Most individuals over the age of 60 aren't out hooking up with new partners every weekend. Yet the biggest concern should be the people they have been with in the past. They may have been exposed to a sexually transmitted diseases such as HIV from a partner they were once with. They aren't able to share that information with you as they don't know it themselves. That is just too big of a risk to take.

Should you decide to be part of a committed relationship when you are over 60 with one partner, that is great. You both should be tested for sexually transmitted diseases though. The time frame for additional testing will depend on how much time has passed since each of you has been with someone else. Your medical professionals can provide all of that information for you.

Only after you get go ahead for the doctor can you stop using protection with that partner. You need to decide on the level of trust you have with that person though. Infidelity is a common issue in our society for people of all ages, not just over 60. If you are worried in the least that you may be exposed to anything due to that issue you need to continue using protection.

It is very naïve to assume that because you aren't a spring chicken anymore that you don't have to worry about the risk of sexually transmitted diseases. There is no discrimination from them based upon your age. Approximately 20% of the population that has tested positive for HIV is over 60 years of age. In at least half of the cases it is believed that they were exposed to the virus by engaging in unprotected sex after the age of 60.

Some individuals of this age group feel it is disrespectful to bring up the use of condoms. They don't want to offend potential partners so they don't even bring it up. Yet if you aren't able to discuss the issue of safe sex with someone you plan to be intimate with then it is best to avoid such activity with them all together.

Others simply don't realize they are still at risk at their age. There has been a great deal of information and education offered on the topic in the last 20 years. This was implemented as the number of individuals over 60 years of age with sexually transmitted diseases was on the rise for several years in a row.

The highest rate of sexually transmitted diseases among adults of this age group is found in male to male relationships. However, those that involve two females or one male and one female are also at risk too. There has been a myth in society that doesn't seem to go away that only homosexual males are at risk of contracting a sexually transmitted disease in their older years. Everyone is at risk and so you should assume that anyone you are going to have sex with could possible have such infections to pass on to you. Some of them may know about it but others don't and you need to not take such a risk.

When you are in your 60's, you still have plenty of life ahead of you to enjoy. A healthy sex life should be a an enjoyable part of that life. However, you do need to be very realistic about the risk of sexually transmitted diseases. You don't want to have something like that affect the quality of the remainder of life you have in front of you.

CONCLUSION

Everything you have just read should, hopefully, provide a decent crash course on the subject of living a rewarding sex life past the age of sixty in today's fast paced society, but, as no book can accurately predict every last one of its reader's specific needs, it's important to keep reading. Most bookstores have an entire section devoted to books on sex, with entire shelves dedicated specifically to the subjects just touched upon in this book.

One of the generally accepted wrongs of today's western culture is the tendency to disregard the elderly, to ignore and exclude anyone over sixty from the aspects of life that are so important to the rest of us. In spite of the general assumption that "geezers don't have sex", for many, sex becomes even more important past a given age. What better way to invigorate yourself and declare to the world that you're not nearly finished than to live a more satisfying sex life than nine out of ten people have amassed the life experience to maintain?

To those who give up on having great sex as soon as the hurdle of age is thrown in front of them, and opt to just wait the rest of their lives out, well, with current medical technology as it is, they might be in for a heck of a wait. There is no worse time than right now to give up on living a healthy and rewarding sex life.

Looking to get your hands on more great books?

Come visit us on the web and check out our giant collection of books covering all categories and topics. We have something for everyone!

http://www.kmspublishing.com

KMS Publishing.com

Made in the USA
Lexington, KY
30 October 2012